Eyes have seen Ears have heard
The Whole Story

Clifford Leon Sheffield, Poet
Introducing
Poet Preston Sheffield

The Whole Story

Eyes have seen Ears have heard
The Whole Story
Clifford Leon Sheffield
Preston Sheffield

ISBN 978-0-9976535-0-2

Copyright 2020
Clifford Leon Sheffield
Preston Sheffield and Cheudi Publishing
First Printing Summer 2020

Printed in the USA
10 9 8 7 6 5 4 3 2 1

The Whole Story

Contents

Dedication

Part I
Poems by Clifford Leon Sheffield

Part II
Poems by nephew Preston Sheffield

Dedication

This book of poems is dedicated to my wife Earline, my children, my grandchildren and my entire extended family. Once we know the "Whole Story" we can live our best stories.

The Whole Story

Part I

Poems by Clifford Leon Sheffield

About The Poet
Clifford Leon Sheffield

Clifford Leon Sheffield is one of ten children (eight boys and two girls) born to Preston and Ella Rene Sheffield. He grew up in Terrell Texas and the Oak Cliff section of Dallas, Texas. After graduation from Kennedy High School, he joined the Military (Air Force) following in the footsteps of his older brothers Charles Preston (Army) and Carl Lester (Air Force), and father Preston (Army). He then returned to Dallas after serving his country where he met and married his wife Earlene. They have been married for over thirty years.

The Whole Story
Clifford Leon Sheffield

There once was a Dragon named Satan who
took a third of the Angels in Heaven
who told them GOD was just hate'n and
controlled them Twenty-Four Seven.

So there was a war in Heaven between Satan, his
Angels and against GOD.
Satan wanted to be in charge of Heaven because He
thought he could do a better Job.

GOD pummeled old Satan and his Army of Angels
he banished them from Heaven to Earth.
Old Satan never gave up though... he kept planning
and scheming for all his worth.

GOD created a man to carry out His Will ...and
named His creation Adam.
He placed Adam in a garden and gave him dominion
over all that his human mind could fathom.

God told Adam "You're in charge of this world. Just
always do what I tell you.
Do these things and I will never forsake or fail you."

GOD looked down on Adam and saw that he was
lonely with no one of his Kind to Relate.

So GOD put Adam to Sleep and took out his Rib
...and created a woman as his Mate.

Adam was happy and content and thanked God for
the woman he'd received.
GOD said "That's good" as He looked down on them
and called the woman Eve.

All the while old Satan was lurking in the garden
watching GOD's Plan Take Shape.
He thought to himself... 'How can I use these two to
finally take GOD's place?'

The old dragon made a plan, so in the garden he
took a stand to bring down man for Evil's Sake.
He took to the Trees and appeared to Eve in the
form of a Serpent called a Snake.

The Snake beguiled Eve and she began to follow his
lead. Just like the 'Pied-Piper's flute.
The Snake said "Now madam... you convince Adam
to eat of The Forbidden Fruit."

They ate of The Fruit, defied GOD to His face and
followed Satan down the road to destruction.
GOD removed His hand of protection as they fell
from grace because they failed to follow God's
Instruction.

On that day Satan took control of this world. And
He controls it to this very day.
He takes control of our minds his every wish, we
obey.

The Whole Story

Satan has disciples just like Jesus did. They
worship and follow him to the Death.
They are some of the ones who are in charge of our
government who we think are looking out for our
safety and Health.

If they say go to war... Then to war we go like
puppets on a string.
We fight and we die and don't even know that our
lives to them don't mean a thing.

Satan and his Cohorts work very hard ...keeping us
confused without exception.
He uses GOD's Ideas ...and distorts them to hide his
deep deception.

He invades our minds at an early age to ingrain his
constitution...
by infiltrating our Church and our educational
institution.

Old Satan knows his Days are numbered and his
time is about to run out.
Soon Jesus will return riding a White Horse ...A
sword in his mouth.

Christ will bind old Satan. Throw him into the
bottomless pit and dispel all our fears.
The Chosen of Christ will serve as Kings and Priests
and He will reign Lord of Lords and King of Kings for
the next One Thousand years.

The Whole Story

At the end of One Thousand years Satan is released ...for a Short Time to continue his endeavor.
Then GOD will cast him into The Lake of Fire where he will be tormented forever and ever...

A Government of the People
Clifford Leon Sheffield

A government of the People, for the people
and by the People no Longer exists.
If you think your vote counts, you're
wrong. No matter how hard you persist.

They just keep on stringing you along.
They gradually condition your mind to
accept whatever they say.
They make you believe it's what's best for
you. They make sure nothing is clear and
every issue is grey.

You're confused and not sure of what to
do they fuel both sides of every issue.
There's lot of showmanship and hoop-to-
do and then discard your opinion like
used tissue.

Then they tell you how much they care.
Every issue is ready to share decided
before it ever comes for a vote.
A system that keeps people divided and at
each other's throat.

The Whole Story

A people divided is easy to control,
because they have no foundation.
If truth be told, they use this technique in
every city, state and nation.

They exploit every weakness we have. They
control us on every level.
They get their directions from their leader
as he sits back and laughs. It's the old
dragon, Satan, the Devil.

Two Roads
Clifford Leo Sheffield

The Bible says that the road to destruction
is broad and many there are that will find it.
That road won't lead to God it will only lead to
the one who designed it.

That road to destruction is crowded and worn.
People can't see where it leads.
Most of us are on that road from the day we
are born because we're more concerned with
our wants than we are with our needs.

We're taught from birth that the only thing
that matters is what we want. So we always
spare the rod.
We ignore the list of do's and don'ts handed
down to us from GOD.

The road to Salvation is narrow and few there
are that find it.
This road is as straight as an arrow because
God is The One who outlined it.

The Whole Story

The narrow road is reserved for those who
have faith in God and obey his command.
When we die, the body goes back to the sod.
The Soul stands in judgment even if you don't
understand.

Toxic Mind Pollution
Clifford Leon Sheffield

They use the Media to fill our minds
with toxic garbage.
They bombard us with it day and night
and the younger generation is the primary
target.

Satan has them in his sights. as they
watch their TV and Computer screen.
They are fed a lot of false and misleading
information. They can tell the most
convincing lies that you've ever heard or
seen.

They make you believe they have a real
concern for this nation. They create
problems and then offer up solutions.
These solutions are fake and they
systematically diminish our constitutional
right.
They dishonor the Constitution and
conquer us without a fight.

The Whole Story

We can plainly see there's something
wrong and that it needs to be fixed.
But we can't see that they're the problem
all along.
And that no outside Threat really exist.

By the time we grow-up, there's such an
intelligence gap. The Truth is hard to find.
We've ingested so much toxic crap that we
need a haz-mat suite for our mind.

The problems we must deal with are not
external. They are not strange or odd.
The problems can be solved from now
until eternity. We just need to change our
hearts and turn back to GOD.

Something Is Wrong
Clifford Leon Sheffield

Every day I sit down to watch the news on
TV. I see the same stories over and over
again.
A young teenage kid is shot down at the
local school. No reason... just because
they can.

A young person takes a knife and stabs a
whole family to death. He shows no
respect for life.
Then he turns the knife on himself.

A mother puts her baby into a tub of
boiling hot water and leaves him to boil
like a stew.
She's angry at 'the baby's father.' So... this
is all she can think to do...

When you see on the news these things
happening everyday you wonder... what's
going on?
GOD made a plan from which we've all
gone astray. We must know that
something is definitely wrong.

The Whole Story

The Only Role Model
Clifford Leon Sheffield

Jesus came as an example of how
we are to live and how we are to treat our
fellowman.
Every action of Jesus was always to give.
as he walked across the hot and barren
land.

Jesus healed "The Sick and raised The
dead in all the places He went.
The people listened to what he said
Because they believed He was sent.

He was The Word of GOD walking this
earth in human flesh and skin.
He came... a virgin birth... born of Mary
to bear our infirmities and sin.

Everywhere he traveled no matter how he
was treated he did nothing but good for
his fellow man.
We should follow His example and not be
so conceited and do the most good
wherever we can.

The Whole Story

If you're looking for someone to pattern
your life after just pick up your Holy Bible
and read.
Within those pages you'll find Joy and
laughter you'll see that Jesus is the only
role model you will ever need.

GOD Sees You
Clifford Leon Sheffield

When you treat your fellowman with
hatred, resentment and animosity,
Regardless of how he treats you,
God sees you.

When you spread lies and rumors about
others, even though they're not true
God sees you.

When you take advantage, or use everyone
to achieve success in whatever you do.
GOD sees you.

When you take another person's life with a
gun or a knife, because of incorrect
assumptions that you drew...
GOD sees you.

GOD also sees you when you extend a
helping hand to help your fellowman with
whatever problem he's trying to get
through.

The Whole Story

When you love your fellowman and do all you can GOD sees that too.
As you choose your path in life from the things you understand how do you want GOD to see you?

Discipline
Clifford Leon Sheffield

Parents give children everything their little
heart's desire. While overlooking the
things they really need.
When a Child does something good, the
praises couldn't be higher. But the praises
keep on coming, even if The Child acts like
a demon seed.

If you praise a child for doing wrong as
well as for doing right, how can that child
grow up morally strong?
If there is nothing wrong in their sight
and you let your child get away with
anything they want.

That's not showing Love. It's indifference
at best. If you don't teach your child
discipline they'll grow into a dunce: who
thinks the world is their oyster and
to hell with all the rest.

When you raise a child with no discipline
or self control you do no Justice to that
child.
The child never grows up he just grows
out of control and wild.

GOD grants us children to nurture, love, and teach.
Not to wait on them hand and foot.
You're the one who helps them set the goals they want to reach.

Keep them grounded like a root. You can let your child run wild and be totally out of control, or you can instill discipline into his life as he grows.
Remember, GOD made you responsible for those little souls. So whatever you do don't let Satan determine how that Life goes.

The Whole Story

What Do You Think
Clifford Leon Sheffield

Do you think GOD will go on, letting us
Spit in His face?
Do you think He'll keep letting us ignore
every commandment He ever gave us?
Do you think He'll keep letting us take
advantage of His Grace.
Do you Think He'll keep letting us ignore
the fact That He sent His Son to save us?

Do you Think GOD is sitting in heaven
watching us destroy everything He
created?
Do you Think He's watching evil run
through this world.
Even mankind itself is threatened to be
eliminated.

How long do you think he'll let us get away
with the total lack of respect we've shown
Him.
How long before we realize that our
conduct is not O.K, and our Lives depend
on Him.

The Whole Story

If we look back through history for those
in the past; those who severed their
spiritual link, GOD said the last shall be
the first and the first shall be the last.
That's true, no matter what we think.

The Whole Story

A Savior Rises
Clifford Leon Sheffield

They beat him, they whipped him they tore the
clothes from his back...
Jesus never said a mumbling word. He did that for
us because he loves us like that.

A love we didn't really deserve. We turned away
from GOD in the garden and lost our connection.
Satan quickly took advantage of that. We were at
Satan mercy, without GOD's hand of Protection.

Satan knew that he could trick us into thinking we
were all that. We felt we didn't need GOD
anymore, so we turned away.
We broke the covenant GOD made with us GOD
blessed us with all that we needed from the very
first day.

But we let Satan convince us that he's the one to
trust. We needed a redeemer.
Satan thought he could take GOD's place but he
was just a dreamer.

The bible says separation from GOD is sin.
That's what happened to us in the garden.
GOD refused to let Satan win. He sent Jesus as our
pardon.

The Whole Story

The bible says the wages of sin is death.
So by right, we should all be lost
but it was Jesus who paid our debt
when they nailed him to the cross.

When Jesus died, he made a decision
to permanently put death away.
We only have to confess and repent
because he rose again on the third day.

The Whole Story

A Tribute to Mothers
Clifford Leon Sheffield

A mother is blessed with the most important job in
the world.
 It starts with giving birth..
Mothers are responsible for every little boy and girl.
Without mothers, they'd never be born on this earth.

Birthing a child is only the start.
The work has just begun
And although the father is there to do his part
A mother's work is never done.

Unlike a father, whose role is to provide and to
protect.
A mother's role is to nurture and to teach.
Although the father is there to guide and direct
it's the mother's encouragement that gets them to
the goals they want to reach.

A child's early year are spent predominately
with its mother.
That's where it learns the importance of Loving and
Forgiving.
The child forms a bond with the mother like no
other.
While the Father is out there somewhere trying to
make a Living.

The Whole Story

I'm not saying a father's role is not important also.
We all have to have food and Shelter whatever we
do.
It's the Mother who shapes Little Minds as they
grow. So your future is all up to you.

The Whole Story

Live Your Own Life
Clifford Leon Sheffield

Do what you Love and Love what you do.
Enjoy Life while you can.
Always remember *"To Thine Own-self Be True."*
Don't follow the dreams of some other man.

Use the mind God gave you to map out a" Plan for
your Life." Don't do it anyone else's way.
You determine how you spend your 'Nine to Five.'
You'll be happy every day.

Don't choose a job just because it pays more.
Choose one that makes you feel happy and fulfilled.
Don't choose a job where every day is just a bore.
Choose one where being there every day is a Thrill.

Working Twenty years on a job you hate
Can make you unpleasant and uptight…
While working on a job you enjoy and appreciate
May fill you're your life with happiness and delight.

Happiness or Unhappiness…?   The choice is yours.
Don't leave it all to Chance.
Life will provide open doors.
It's up to you to Retreat or Advance.

The Whole Story

The Whole Story

Follow Your Heart
Clifford Leon Sheffield

Stop. Look and Listen. Then Think before you
Start. Use your eyes. Use your Ears and then Use
Your Heart.
When your eyes are *tempted* by things that look
good to you when your ears hear things that sound
right. Follow your heart.

It'll Tell you what to do. It'll lead you to God's
Holy Light. GOD deals with your heart.
He fills it full of His pure Love. You'll realize it if
you're smart

His Love is something you can never have too
much of. God filled your heart with His pure
Love for a reason.
 He wants you to spread it around. Not just during
the Holiday Season.

Spread Love every time your feet hits the ground
and sow seeds of Love wherever you go.
Always water and nourish The Seed.
More Love will always grow and provide all The
Things you need.

The Whole Story

Follow your heart as it leads you to God.
Find The Love He wants you to share.
Align yourself with him like 'Two Peas in a Pod."
Life will be better for everyone everywhere.

The Whole Story

Brain Washing
Clifford Leon Sheffield

Don't believe what your eyes See. Don't Trust what
your mine thinks.
Your thoughts might not be your own. We are
bombarded with all sorts of mind control techniques
before we develop our own instincts.

They get inside our heads and confuse us until we
don't know right from wrong. They have control of
all media publications all educational institutions
and religions.
They control every government on this earth. They
are the biggest influence in all our decisions.

They've been in our heads since birth. They depend
on our parents who were brain washed before us so
they raised and trained us their way.
Our parents, who Love us and will do anything for
us have no clue they control everything we do and
say.

The Whole Story

When ideas form in our heads they're based on information from them. They use the media to implant ideas in our mind.
They direct our lives like a Hollywood movie while we think it's all our doing and everything is just fine.

Since they control our minds and shape our thoughts. We're so consumed by what we are taught and we never know we're being controlled.
Until we turn back to God... The Creator of us all... He'll show us wonders and signs. When we listen to God and begin to answer His call...

And Let Him Control our minds the state of the world. This world is in a state of misunderstanding, misleading, misdirection, and missing the mark.
We turn a deaf ear to all of GOD's instructions. Because of this our children are left totally in the dark.

Without a clue as to how to deal with Satan's seductions. we've turned away from Jesus and started to look for Salvation in other places.
We've left ourselves open to Satan's advances. We're following a plan that has no bases.

The Whole Story

A plan that eliminates all our chances. Satan takes advantage of our misguided minds and our misguided hearts.
He uses our confusion to control us where obedience to God ends is where obedience to Satan starts.

He comforts us with lies that makes us think he's there to console us. Don't let Satan trick you into following the ways of the world.
You really have nothing to gain. Just like water draining from a sink it goes round and round in a swirl.

If we would just stop and think! We'd See this world circling down the drain. Turn back to GOD right away.
Follow The Example of Abel, not Cain you can be Saved today.

The Whole Story

The Whole Story

The Real Deal
Clifford Leon Sheffield

If you believe there is a GOD. You're Right.
You don't even have to think about it.
Just Look around you at everything in sight.
It makes you wonder how anyone could ever doubt
it.

The earth gets its Light, Heat and Energy for the
Sun.
This big ball of Light in The Sky.
You must ask yourself, where did it come from.
Who put it there and why.

The Sun didn't just spring up out of nowhere.
It's existence is no accident.
God took great patience and care.
He made sure The Sun served The Purpose he
meant.

There's The Moon and Stares to guide us by night
Whenever we are not facing The Sun.
Their majestic beauty outshines everything in sight.
God planned it from before time begun.

The Whole Story

God created this planet, from the mountains…to
the valleys and the Seas.
There was never any big bang God created it all.
God created everything that grows on this planet…
from the smallest to the tallest trees.

God created everything to be at our beckon call.
God created the animals, the fishes, the insects and
the birds. He created them from nothing. Like all
the rest.
God created all these things under our care to put us
through a Test.

God created everything we could ever possibly need
to sustain.
Then He created us. We need to show him his work
was not in vein.

We need to give Him our total unbridled Trust.
Trust in and Love God always. Do This no matter
how you feel.
Don't muddle through life in a daze. Remember that
all God created is Real.

The Whole Story

Satan's Army
Clifford Leon Sheffield

It's Crystal Clear that Satan and his minions are
calling all the shots.
They're masters of deceit and manipulation.
My personal opinion is… you only have to connect
the dots.

When you do, you'll see the pattern of total control
over our entire situation' They control us indirectly
through the organizations that are served.
The government, the media, the religions, the
educational systems and everything we trust.
These organizations were established to provide all
the things we felt we deserved.

Instead we wound up serving them, instead of them
serving us. Our government is no longer a
government it has taken more of a corporate role.
They don't care how our tax money is spent, when
waste is really the goal.

They manufacture a problem to spend more money
on. This year so they can charge you more taxes
next year. They extort our hard earned cash.

The Whole Story

The taxes we pay and our charitable donations are motivated by fear. And they keep starting foundations where they hide their stash.

Our government is not the elected officials we cast our votes for. They are the powers behind them that we don't see.
They are not the ones we campaigned and spoke about. They are the ones who control all the banks And have the Leverage to control you and me.

All our sources of information, entertainment and communication are provided and maintained by them. They always know what is on our minds because they put it there.
They determine what we are thinking and how we feel everywhere.

They use the media to invade our minds like hypnotist.
They plant suggestions, ideas and thoughts in our minds. They guide and advise us like therapists.

They use words and Symbols and Signs. The media is one of the main Tools of Satan and his army. They use it to control our lives.
Whenever you feel your life is getting a little stormy remember Satan and his army will soon meet their demise.

The Whole Story

Our schools have become nothing more than
indoctrination centers, where they program our
minds.
The programming goes from pre-school through
college. They entangle our minds like winding
vines.

They fill us up with all kinds of useless knowledge
with our minds all filled with a lot of stuff we can
never use.
We don't have room for any useful information.
The deeper the programming, the more of us we
loose.

We're not the people God envisioned at our
creation. With everyone programmed to simply
follow directions.
Control is now automatic. It's getting harder and
harder to see the man God created when we look in
the mirror at our reflections.

God should be the only one programming our
minds. And that my friend is emphatic. We all
practice some kind of religion.
Our decision and the one we need and choose to
believe is that someone higher than ourselves. But
the decisions are not always ours in the end.

The Whole Story

Satan has his minions in our churches who Lead
God's people astray.
He can do this because he is the master of deceit.
And through our religious leaders Satan controls us
from day to day.

His Army never 'Lets Up' because he cannot accept
defeat. We are so caught up in rituals and traditions
that we neglect to call on God every day.
Before you make any decisions remember… It's
always smart to find out what GOD has to say.

We shouldn't let Satan use our organizations to
control us. We should turn to GOD for guidance
and hope.
He's the only one we can count on to Love and
Control us as we navigate Life's Slippery Slope.

Satan has an army. It's true. And it seems like they
are winning The Battle.
But we never give up on God no matter and
whatever we do. In The End Times there'll be no
fence to straddle.

The Whole Story

With God in our lives Satan does not stand a
chance. He might appear to be a bright and shining
star.
Satan might win a few battles as he makes his
advances. But he knows he will never ever win the
War.

Satan has his army all around us, everywhere we
turn. He cannot leave us the way he finds us. He
injects his influence into all we know. Some of our
leaders have been drafted into his army and every
move they make is at his command.
Whenever life gets a little stormy some may
Turn to Satan instead of God for a helping hand.

Satan makes all the decisions we think we are
making. All the options are provided by him. Our
will is so weak we can be His for the taking.
Satan controls us at his whim.

God made us to be like Him… Loving, Caring,
Compassionate and Strong. He sent His Son Jesus
to tell us that he is coming back again and that it
won't be long. If we are smart, we will turn back to
God right now.

The Whole Story

The Whole Story

Technical Problems
Clifford Leon Sheffield

We have everything at our fingertips
No effort is required.
We don't even have to split our lips
To have everything that's desired

Technology is so advanced we can have everything
on demand.
We don't even have to take a chance
Because anything we can't achieve
Our Technology can.

Thinking has become obsolete.
Nobody does it anymore.
It's as though we think our brains will
Over-heat if we let one thought pass the front door

Why bother thinking, when technology does all the
work.
We can access any information we want
Through our telephones.
We can access any information
We want through our telephones.

The Whole Story

We can spy on our friends and neighbors
And we don't even have to Lurk
We can see everything they do with
Our surveillance drones.

Technology makes us lazy and
complacent about everything.
We don't want to work for what we get.
If we continue on this path, we'll
Soon start to sink.
We'll find ourselves in regret.

We must understand that total access to
Everything we want comes with a price.
Nothing man offers is free.
Before you surrender your future to Technology
Please heed this advice.
If you want to unlock the mysteries
Of his world, only God has the Key.

God created it all in the first place.
He's someone we can always Trust.
He's not out there somewhere in cyber space
He Lives inside each one of us.
Technology was not meant to own us
Remember. GOD Created Technology Too!

Don't Settle
Clifford Leon Sheffield

It would be wonderful if all The People
Of The World were on The same page.
If we were all on one accord.
Satan would be in such a rage
If we all turned back to our Savior and Lord

There are two forces in this world
That controls our Thoughts and our Lives
One of hose forces is Satan,
The other is our Creator.
It won't be long before the end Time arrives.

We each have to decide for ourselves
Which of those forces is greater.
Satan can grant you everything you want
In this world.
Because this world is his domain.
He can give you diamonds and pearls

But anything he grants you is always
Temporary and in Vain.
Satan can only give you things
That Won't Last.
Things That will Soon pass away.
GOD can free you from your past

The Whole Story

And grant you happiness every day.
God can offer you Life without end.
Satan can't do that at his best.
While you're out there searching for
a friend.
Why Settle for anything Less?

The Whole Story

Real Love
Clifford Leon Sheffield

When GOD molded man into His
image and after His likeness
That is to look like Him and to be
like Him.
GOD filled man with His brightness
so that his outlook wouldn't be so dim.
That's real Love.

GOD provided man with everything
he needed to sustain and maintain
himself.
All man had to do is not be conceited
and show Love to everyone else.
That's real Love.

You don't Love with your Mind.
You Love with your Heart.
Because your mind can be impersonal
and cold.
Deep inside is where Love Starts,
where it feeds and nourishes the Soul.
That's real Love.

The Whole Story

GOD Loves us still
though we've disobeyed his Will.
We've turned our backs on Him
a countless number of times.
God said don't hate, steal or kill.
He expects the same from all man-kind.
That's real Love.

Fill your heart with love to be like GOD.
Don't worry about what others do
even if GOD uses the rod.
Love will find them just like it found you.
That's real Love.

Mind Control
Clifford Leon Sheffield

Two objects cannot occupy the same
Space at the same time.
That's a Law of nature and a scientific Truth.
If you want to easily control a people
You must first infiltrate their minds.
The most efficient way to do that is
to start with The Youth.

You must control the Educational System
from the Bottom to top
You must erase everything they've
Learned so far.
You must bombard them with all
Your theories and ideas non-stop.
Make them so confused that they don't
Know who or what they are.

Certain information must be purged from
People's minds.
You must replace it with whatever
You want them to believe.
Hen in due time
Those people won't know
They've been deceived.

The Whole Story

You should mold and shape their minds
while they're young.
Continue this process until they are adults.
When you infiltrate a people's minds
It's easy to string them along.
Total control is the result.

When you determine what a human mind
thinks about.
If every thought is for your satisfaction
You control that mind without a doubt.
As those thoughts translate into actions
Everything those people do is decided by you.
They don't have an idea or opinion of their own.
They really don't have a clue.

They don't know the difference between
Right and wrong.
When GOD created man in the beginning
He only had to remember one thing.
That is to do everything GOD said.
If he had stayed focused on that
He wouldn't be dangling at the end
Of Satan's String.
He wouldn't be spiritually dead.

The Whole Story

Satan killed The GOD spirit in all of us.
He tricked us into Thinking
that we are alone.
He took over our minds without a fuss.
He made us forget about The One to
whom we belong.

GOD is our creator and our protector.
With Satan we'll all be condemned.
GOD is our director.
When we remember that
We will all turn back to Him.
Stop letting Satan control your mind.
Turn back to GOD right away
We are living right now in The End Time.
Keep GOD in your Life Every Day.

The Whole Story

The Whole Story

Big Brother
Clifford Leon Sheffield

No matter how easy or good we have it
We always want things better
If we spot a short cut we always grab it
We even want our water wetter

We want everything handed to us on a silver platter
We don't want to have to work for a thing
Where these things come from or how they are
Acquired does not matter

As long as we don't have to Lift a finger.
Every bit of technology that comes along
We can't wait to buy into.
Never realizing that big brother doesn't
Think it's wrong to use that same technology
To monitor and control everything we do

If we keep letting the system determine
How and what we think
and how we treat each other.
We'll lose control of our lives before
We can blink.
We'll be totally under the control
of big brother.

The Whole Story

Big brother doesn't care what we
Think or how we feel
He just wants to have Total Control.
He uses technology as a mental Link

O make us willingly do what we're told.
Big Brother can control us, because
He knows how to play on our Laziness
and our greed.
As Long as he keeps our heads in a fog
Of haziness
We'll continue to Follow His Lead.

The Whole Story

Self-Destruct
Clifford Leon Sheffield

Sin is Dynamite and Satan is the fuse.
But The fuse can never self ignite.
He needs someone to use.

Satan has no power, yet we obey him on demand.
We know that Satan will devour
But we don't know our fate is in our hands.

The fuse can never be lit until we let it.
We're always just fine until we do.
We must remember That GOD is in Charge
and don't forget it.

He'll always do what is best for you.
Satan can get into your head.
He can make you forget about GOD.
He can make you forget what GOD said.

And totally give Him the nod.
You can keep GOD in your daily Life.
You can Let GOD determine your conduct
or you can Let The Fuse of Satan
inite and Totally Self-destruct.

The Whole Story

The Whole Story

Satan Goes Hunting
Clifford Leon Sheffield

Satan is going hunting all over this nation
He's looking to secure as any souls as he can.
His weapons are lies, deceit, and manipulation.
He seeks control over all the peoples in all
the Land.

He Traps His prey by appearing to be GOD.
He uses GOD's Ideas as his own.
The people can't see through his facade.
We can't see that the path he's leading us
down is wrong.

Satan steals GOD's plans and alters
them to fit his needs.
We don't understand, so we follow
Wherever he leads

Don't get snared by Satan's web of deceit.
Keep a close relationship with GOD.
Study GOD's word everyday of the week.
GOD's Word will expose this fraud.

Stick with GOD. He'll give all that
your heart is wanting.
Just remember,,, where ever you trod
Satan is still out there hunting.

The Whole Story

The Whole Story

Socially Unequal
Clifford Leon Sheffield

The concept of equal opportunity has
Never been a reality in This nation.
It has always been a system of social classes.
The lower classes have always suffered
degradation.

While the privileged few rule over and
controll the masses.
They tell you, as long as you work hard
you can be whatever you want to be.
That whatever you want to become
in Life is up to you.
They keep you working so hard you can barely see
and you are forever stuck in the Class you are born
into.

They tell you get an education
you can determine your fate.
When you finally find out that what you really got
was an indoctrination
by then it's way too Late.

The Whole Story

No matter how hard you work, you'll never be one
of them.
Your future has been framed and sealed.
No matter how much education you think you have,
Your chances are very slim
That promise of equality you thought you had
is just not real.

Don't go on Thinking you'll be accepted and
embraced.
Don't set yourself up for The Fall.
The ruling elite are too cowardly to
tell you to your face.
You'll never be accepted at all.

Stop Looking for approval from the oppressor.
He'll have to answer to GOD sooner or later.
Don't look for answers from some professor.
Turn your heart back to the Creator.

Blessing
Clifford Leon Sheffield

B – is for your Belief in GOD's Power and Strength

L – is for Loving Him with all your Heart

E – is for everlasting Life at His Judgment

S – is for The Salvation That Sets you apart

S – is for standing Tall Though the World tries to beat you down

I - is for The Inspiration you get from His Love

N – is for The New Life that by His Blessing is found

G – is for GOD who watches over us from Heaven above

This Spells Blessing… something each of us need. It's not something we deserve. God grants us a blessing through The Blood of His Seed.

And The Least we can do is Serve Him.

The Whole Story

Be A Sponge
Clifford Leon Sheffield

You might read your Bible everyday
You might be able to quote Chapters and Verses.
But do you really get what The Word Says?
Do you really understand all The Blessings and The
Curses?

The Bible Is GOD'S Written Word.
You Must Embrace and Endear it.
Just like a mother bird Lovingly Feeds her baby
birds.
The Bible feeds our spirit.

Your spirit needs to be nourished just like your
body and your mind.
They all need time to grow and mature.
You can't keep your spiritual growth in a bind
and expect your body and mind to be secure.

Don't just take baby steps when you pick up
your Bible to read.
Take a giant Lunge.
Then GOD will Bless you with all you need.
When you absorb him like a Sponge.

The Whole Story

The Whole Story

Don't Count GOD Out
Clifford Leon Sheffield

When your Faith is wavering because you think
GOD let you down.
When your faith is slowly turning to doubt
When you pray and pray and still no answers are
found.
Don't count GOD out.

GOD knows your every thought.
He sees your selfishness and your greed.
He may not grant you all the things you think
he ought.
But He makes sure you always get the things you
need.
Don't count GOD out.

Satan can make you believe that you have the right
to complain and pout.
But before you let Satan step in and have your
whole life re-arranged
Don't count GOD out.

Don't try to handle your problems all alone
and when they get to be too much
God already knows what they are all about.
Let Him handle it with his tender loving touch.
Never count GOD out.

The Whole Story

The Willie Lynch Plan
Clifford Leon Sheffield

There once was a Slave owner by the name of
Willie Lynch
Who penned a Letter to other Slave Owners of his
time.
The Letter stated that future control of your slaves
will be a cinch.
Just take The Chains off their hands and feet
and put them on their minds.

If you train a generation of slaves to go to
The back door, Willie said.
After a couple of generations, you won't have to
train them anymore.
The chains will no Longer be on their hands and
feet, but on their minds instead.

If you condition their minds over a period of time
They will submit and conform to your will.
As history unfolds you'll have full control.
Your wishes, they'll be eager to fulfill.

The Whole Story

This technique has been adapted by the powers that be, and is now being used on the whole population.

The affect is so subtle that the people can't see as it is passed on to the next generation.

With chains firmly on their minds they're just standing in line to please the master however they can.

Their free will is gone. They have no will of their own all because of the Willie Lynch Plan.

The Whole Story

No Strength of Our Own
Clifford Leon Sheffield

Human weakness is a condition we all suffer from
Sometimes we can't control it on our own
Help shouldn't come from just anyone.
But from The One To whom we belong.

We all have Things we crave to much
And we don't do well without it.
But the one's we go to for help becomes a crutch.
They can't do a thing about it.

The so called experts can't help with your problem.
It's not Like going to a physician.
They can't help you solve them
When they have The same condition.

You can want something so bad that when you
can't get it the evil in you emerges.
The experts tell you that you have a disease
because you can't control your urges.

You have a weakness, not a disease.
You can get things back under control.
Just get down on your knees, pray to GOD,
And you'll see miracles unfold.

The Whole Story

From the drugs we take, the food we eat,
the Things we do that we call fun.
We over indulge in everything is sight.
We just can't seem to say "I'm done."

We can't help our human weakness.
We are human after all.
We can always use GOD's strength don't ever seek
less.
GOD's strength will always make us Stand Tall.

When we try to do things in our own strength
we'll find that we really have none.
Any victories we claim were won by Consent
given by the all powerful one.

It Don't Work Like That
Clifford Leon Sheffield

People think GOD is here to serve us.
We think we make rules that govern our lives.
We adore our money that has the words
In God We Trust on it.
Seems like we'll keep minimizing GOD
Until Judgment day arrives.

We ignore all GOD's Statutes and Laws.
We make up our own rules.
We convince our children that to follow
The example of Jesus is a lost cause.
We even teach that crap in our public schools.

When we don't choose Jesus as our example to
follow everything we do will fall flat.
Every idea we have will be empty and hollow.
Because it just don't work like that.

We never teach our children about GOD.
They learn to feed their egos and their greed.
In raising our children they never get
The discipline they need.

The Whole Story

We fill our children's heads with lies
Telling them "a mind is a terrible thing to waste."
We haven't been able to open our eyes since
Adam fell from grace.

When we get down on our knees to GOD
and have a little chat.
We'll wake up and realize it just
doesn't work like that.

We think we can lie, cheat, steal and kill
and GOD will just look the other way.
Everything we do that's not in GOD's will
we'll have to pay for someday.

Our leaders we think we choose
really don't care.
They believe they have nothing to lose.
And the masses suffer unaware.

We don't know that it just doesn't matter
what we say, what we do, where our heads are,
we can spew out all kinds of puffed up chatter
But it just doesn't work like that.

The Whole Story

If you're interested in how it really does work,
and what GOD has to say.
Don't just pick up your Bible for Church on
Sundays. Pick it up every day.

The Whole Story

Lost In the Wilderness
Clifford Leon Sheffield

The Israelites wondered in the wilderness for forty years. They no longer wanted to follow the GOD of Moses.
They began to listen to the pagan voices in their ears and missed the blessings right under their noses.

GOD released them from four hundred years of bondage and servitude.
He promised them a land of milk and honey but as soon as the journey began to get a little rough they started to give GOD a lot of attitude.

They cried out to Aaron, "We're too tired! We've had enough" We're tired, hungry, and we have no food!"
GOD sent a cloud to shade them by day and a pillar of fire to guide them by night.
But they still complained every step of the way and became afraid whenever Moses wasn't in sight.

The Whole Story

GOD sent down food… manna from heaven.
He knew they would need it to keep up their strength.
But the people stayed in a foul mood and kept complaining wherever they went.

While Moses was in the mountain receiving GOD's Law the people lost their fear of GOD's wrath.
They gathered up all the gold they saw and formed a golden calf.

Moses came down from the mountain GOD's law in his hand.
He found the people worshiping the calf made from the gold.
Moses took a very firm stand.
He broke the calf into pieces and destroyed the mold.

The people were disappointed, confused,
they thought GOD had lied.
They didn't understand their disbelief had begun to show, and their faith would be tried.

We are in that same situation today.
We don't understand that our faith will be tested.
GOD will never turn us away.
He only needs to know that He can count on
the people in which His time has been invested.

The Whole Story

Satan has us all mixed up. He has us caught in an optical and mental allusion.
If we don't begin to recognize the difference between what's right and corrupt we will continue to be lost in a wilderness of confusion.

The Whole Story

The Whole Story

After His Likeness
Clifford Leon Sheffield

GOD created man in His own Image and after
his likeness to represent his presence on earth.
Man was to demonstrate his righteousness after
his body was molded from the dirt.

'In His Image' means to Look Like Him…
…A bright and Shining Light.
After His Likeness" is to be like him.
And to always do what's right.

GOD meant for man to rule this world.
He was to rule it the same way GOD would.
GOD would protect man from all danger and perils.
All man had to do was choose to do good.

GOD wanted to conquer Satan through man
and put him back in his place.
But man went away from GOD's plan and
immediately fell from grace.

There is one thing for sure… we must understand
if we don't want things to be so grim
We must return to GOD's Plan
and always be like Him.

The Whole Story

The Whole Story

Credit Where Credit Is Due
Clifford Leon Sheffield

We never give GOD credit when good things
happen to us.
When bad things happen He always gets the blame.
We always want more than what's due us
We do all sort of evil things in His name.

Bad Things happen in our lives because.
What goes around always comes back around.
So it shouldn't be such a big surprise
That happiness can't be found.

We think we have the right to enslave another
people. All in The Name of GOD.
We think we have the right to chain, to whip
And to beat those people
Because GOD said "Don't spare The Rod."

Those words were instructions on how to raise our
children.
It was not permission to abuse another.
'The Rod' GOD spoke of was The Rod of
Discipline.
Without it our children suffer

The Whole Story

With all the cruel and evil things we do in this Life.
GOD still continues to Bless us.
He's waiting for us to start using our Spiritual Drive
and to Stop Letting Satan Possess us.

When we return to GOD where we should have
been all along
then we will begin to do what we were supposed
to.
We'll stop blaming GOD for all that's wrong
and give Credit where Credit is Due.

The Whole Story

Turn Around
Clifford Leon Sheffield

Stop! Stand perfectly still.
Take a good look all around you what do you see?
Do you see people trying to do GOD's Will?
Do you see us being the man that GOD created us
to be?

Do we have Love and forgiveness in our hearts
for our fellow man?
Or are we looking for any opportunity to cheat
and take advantage of him.
Do we look for every opportunity to help
wherever we can?
Or do we abandon The weak and helpless
to sink or swim?

Do we lie, cheat, and steal to acquire
all the things we think we need?
Or do we consider how others might
feel about our selfish greed?
GOD created man in His image
that is to do whatever he would.
GOD is perfect and without blemish
everything He does is for good.

The Whole Story

You can keep letting Satan lead you around by your
nose.
You can keep doing the things you know are wrong.
You can keep riding Satan's high and lows.
Or you can turn back to GOD, where you belong.

The Whole Story

Man Kind
Clifford Leon Sheffield

One person's junk is another person's treasure.
It depends on what you value most.
Each person uses a different value system to
measure.
What looks good to one person, to another might
look gross.

What might be one person's anguish might be
another person's pleasure.
People are different... like flakes of Snow.
No two are ever the same.
This holds true wherever we go.

Though we all seem to be on different pages
And though we've strayed from the oneness of
mind
The truth still rings out through the ages.
We're still part of one mankind.

Though we all have our own separate personalities
we have our own individual ways.
We're still part of GOD's realities that He
created at the beginning of days.

The Whole Story

The Whole Story

Follow the Right Light
Clifford Leon Sheffield

If you think you can trust anyone, you're
naïve.
Our only concern is for self.
GOD is the only one you can believe.
You can't depend on anyone else.

We've strayed from GOD's natural order of
things.
We've followed after Satan's rules.
We've abandoned our roles as kings and
queens.
We've become a world of fools.

We've fallen prey to Satan's Lies.
We've even adopted them as our own.
Still we expect GOD to hear our cries
and save us though we're wrong.

Salvation doesn't cost us anything Jesus
paid for us on the cross
All we have to do is repent and admit that
we are lost.
Use Jesus's life here on earth as your
model.
Love and do good for your fellow man
GOD is not a genie in a bottle.

The Whole Story

He doesn't grant wishes. He makes
commands.
Live your Life the Jesus way.
Don't Lie. Don't Steal. Don't cheat.
Look for ways everyday to lift up,
encourage and motivate everyone you meet.
Stop following Satan salvation is yours.

Do what you know is right.
When you do, GOD will open doors as he
leads you toward The Light.

The Whole Story

Decisions
Clifford Leon Sheffield

You must discipline yourself.
Every decision has an effect.
Every decision must hit 75%
from the procession.

You can't hit them all.
Everyone falls short of His glory.
We all make mistakes;
But that's not a good excuse.

To succeed you must believe
In what choices you make.
Better choices the stronger the outcome
All things revolve around decisions made;

A choice to be wise not foolish
A choice to listen or ignore;
And a choice to love God or not;
Whatever the cost
You make the choice.

The Whole Story

THINK
Clifford Leon Sheffield

Turn back to GOD before it's too late

Hear His word and get rid of hate

Inspire others to participate

Never let Satan instigate

Know that GOD is never late.

The Whole Story

Part II
*Poems by
Nephew Preston Sheffield*

About The Poet
Preston Sheffield

Preston Sheffield (aka Yosef) was born and raised in Dallas, Texas. He is a successful husband, father, businessman, entrepreneur, author and activist. He was educated at Ashford University and acquired a Bachelor's degree in Business. One of his passions is writing poetry and prose.

Be Willing To Die In Order To Live
Preston Sheffield

Then he delivered Him over to them to be crucified. And they took Jesus and led him away. So He went out to the spot called "The Place of the Skull" in Hebrew that is called Golgotha. There they crucified Him and with Him two others, one on either side were dangling between them." (AMP) John 19:16-18

After being beaten, mocked, rejected by his people and being handed over to his enemy, Jesus was led to the site of his crucifixion bearing his own cross. What a Burden it must have been to bear that stake. The strength and endurance it must have taken. But with one goal in mind he took the abuse and overlooked the iniquity (Roman 5:1) in order to reconcile us to the Father because sin separated us from God. How painful this event is and was, he asked (Matthew 10:38, Mark 9:34, Luke 14:27) us to take up our cross and follow Him. But where does he ask us to follow Him. But where does he ask us to follow him? He asks us to follow him to the crucifixion site bearing our own cross. Are you willing to follow in the (1 Peter 2:21) steps of Christ bearing your cross to the site of crucifixion. Are you willing to crucify (Gal 5:24-25) your flesh with its passion, superstition and desires. This will require commitment. It requires us to overlook iniquity. (Proverb 12:16) It requires you to leave vengeance (1 Peter 2:23). It requires you to leave vengeance (1 Peter 2:23) to the Lord who is just. It requires you to do right even when wronged. We must change ourselves from everything that contaminates and defiles the body and Spirit (2 Corinthian 7:1), we must walk in Integrity (Proverbs 13:6) not being committed and to start something and not bring it to completion (Luke 14:28-32). Because to do the contrary is to succumb to the desires of the flesh and the working (Galatians 6: 15:19-26) of the flesh are evident, strife, jealousy, iniquity, envy, idolatry and immorality. Now that we know we must follow Christ to the site of crucifixion and crucify our flesh. Jesus asks us to take one more step. He asks us to die. John 19:30 which says… And He bowed His head and gave up the Spirit. We see that there was no struggle for Christ to hang on to this life because (Matthew10:38, Luke 14:33) "Whoever hates his life will gain life." He was not only willing to lose his life, he was willing to surrender to the Father's Will. In verse (19:32) two men who hung on the cross were not willing to give up the spirit. So their legs were broken bringing forth immediate death. We see many believe who took up their cross and have followed Jesus to Golgotha.

They sat there hanging on the cross, crucifying their flesh but some have not been willing to die. They have not been willing to give up the ghost as Christ did. So they hung there until some terrible event causes them to die. Maybe they lose a family member, maybe it is a divorce or setup. You see the death that Christ died as a way of death to sin (Romans 6:10) and the life He lived, he lived to GOD. Christ calls us to share in His crucifixion; his death and even His Resurrection. (Roman 6:5). He tells us we must (Roman 6:4) be baptized into His death in order that just as He rose, we might live and behave in the newness of life. You see baptism represents death to the old (Luke 12:50), and resurrection to a new life. So the question is... are you willing to die in order to live?

Why is man willing to scream injustice when a person sins against them but are not willing to die to sin which causes turmoil all over the Earth?

The Whole Story

Straw Man
Preston Sheffield

This Nation was built on conquest and Confiscation.
Ruled by Secret Societies who dictate Situations
Buckle up. We are about to have a serious
conversation.
Listen for your enlightenment this is education
85% are slaves on modern day plantations

You thought slavery ended in 1863
thought that the times had ended when blacks
worked for free
It's a new age of slavery you just can't see
Look at the history of what happened in March of
'33

They switched up the game; it's call UCC
During that same year Uncle Sam filed for
bankruptcy
The Depression crippled America economically
So the powers that be declared an emergency

Eliminated our rights
Turned Us to Currency
The Result is the Strawman
he's their property

The Whole Story

Because of the Sheppurt-Towner Maternity Act
Soon as you escape the wound you are under
contract
We're born in a war zone, deadly as mortal combat
They camouflage their nets like a contact

So before you can ask who done that?
You ever wondered why you identify?
A Sleeper-cell invaded, we took a power nap
Our Freedom has been disabled now we're
handicap

The Battle With-in
Preston Sheffield

Blood spills on battlefields like the invasion of
Normandy
War waging within my soul... super natural
anomalies
I remember the day he came... the devil he tempted me
Told me to bow down but I screamed... Blaspheme
So I'm dodging and ducking fiery projectiles
I'm a target, hated cause of my lifestyle
So I'm down on my knees like a praying mantis
Cause my life revolves around the sun just like the
planets

Artifacts
Preston Sheffield

Life is a museum filled with a plethora of artifacts,
from the radiate light of the sun
To the reflection of the moon by night the
roughness of the sea from the rebellions and
revolutions
Who produced off-springs that are free to nurture,
how marvelous, expressive are her ways

Life forms for the darkness,
Life forms for the day's darkness
Life forms for the days.

But what inspires me the most,
The delicate lines that shape your face,
Your personality and skin tone continues to
captivate.

A sparkle in your eyes causes my inner world to
shake,
Shuttering my insecurities, my negativity began to
break,

There's an ache, you are the beat of my heart
Even though I'm surrounded by many artifacts
You are the Greatest Work of Art.

The Whole Story

I am the offspring of my people,
The result of their struggle and sacrifice,
A product of their stubbornness,
A child of destiny, A child of greatness.

The Whole Story

Mirror
Preston Sheffield

No mirror could do you justice
only I can
If you could see you through my eyes
then you'd understand,

What I see, the average man,
cannot realize,
Lusting over your assets and waistline,
blind to the dreams he cannot find,

Talk to me… I have the answer
I'll be your lifeline,
We can share millions of experiences through-out
this life and time

The Whole Story

Diamond Crush
Preston Sheffield

Clear Cut, yet flawless
Your Emerald eyes fade from blue to green
What wisdom lies behind those eyes?

CRUSH

Auburn hair flowing like trees in Autumn
Yet as the seasons change you remain the same-
Time-less…
Timeless as waves in the Sea
Timeless as the darkness of space
Timeless as time itself
Crushed

The Whole Story

Smile
Preston Sheffield

Your Smile,
Calms Raging Winds
Stills eternal turbulence
That life sometimes brings

Your smile
Resembles the Rising Sun
Penetrating dark clouds,
Blinding optical vines

Your Smile
My narcotic of choice
Cloud nine is approaching
And Heaven's not far away

The Whole Story

Black Lotus
Preston Sheffield

When you move are you walking on Air?
Your voice reminds me of a song
that only the soul can hear.
Intelligence and beauty too
Traits clasp within your hand,
Why are you afraid?
Don't they belong to you?
Wamuiru… beautiful black one born from
the rays of the Sun.
You shine brightly in the darkness of ignorance.
Your heart is a garden with rivers
flowing in a desert oasis.

Redemption
Preston Sheffield

-An angel at my best, but a devil at the worst
-My wings took me high pride crushed me to the
earth

-Dwelling with these demons but no one to stay 'em
-Blood in, Blood out. How can I betray 'em

Sometimes I hate 'em. I'll use the sea-legs of
justice to weigh 'em
-A thin line between truth and fake. How do you
measure the balance

-One produce life and the other death, sleepless
nights with no rest
-Preacher says God Loves me and claims I'm
blessed
-So take me to the altar, it's time to confess.

Two Groups
Preston Sheffield

There are two groups, but neither is experiencing
the same consequence of action,
One group is experiencing life, while the other rests
in the flames of purification.
One group is experiencing purity, while the other is
being made pure through the flame.
One group is aware that they have life. The other is
ignorant of the fact that adversity is a means to
purify them. Yet many remain in the flames
 listen close there are two groups. One
experiencing Eden, while the other remains in the
flames of hell.

The Whole Story

Evidence of Hate
Preston Sheffield

If a man attempted to murder you in cold blood,
under no pretence would you call that love or hate.
Your daughter's boyfriend, lover, or husband
abuses her. Is that love or hate?
A person who attempts to do us harm deserve what?
Punishment, Death or What?
It's obvious that all evidence indicates a hate for us.
Can a man or woman say that they love their
spouse, yet cheat on them at the same time?
How is that love?
You say you love your God but you curse Him
when things don't go as planned. Is that love?
Dig Deeper… What about love or hate of self?
You say you love yourself, but your every action is
evidence of hate for self.
Inhaled a pack of cigarettes that cost darn near ten
bucks! Now you are broke and unhealthy.
Is that love?
You are dressed in the latest fashions, but you are
behind on your rent. Is that love?
Don't you know that the food, drugs, cigarettes, and
alcohol producers are banking on your death,
banking on your ignorance. Lenders are
banking on your financial debt. Cancer was linked
to burned tobacco between 1920 and 40, but
did the production end? CIA trading guns

The Whole Story

for drugs in the 70's and 80's, then took those same
drugs and introduced them to urban communities
while declaring a war on drugs. Is that Love?
We kill ourselves with our diet and lifestyle, while
the health care industry charges us high Fees...
profiting off our hate of self. So in every
circumstance ask yourself... "Is it love or hate?

\

The Whole Story

Sun
Preston Sheffield

We are the rising Sun.
Rose from the darkness as the night begun
There are several spectrums of light a golden dawn.
We are heavyweights in this game of life
Weighed in metric tons
We're spinning on our axis
Considered great like Cassius,
All formed from clay,
Ashes to Ashes! Dust to Dust!
Alchemist can turn trash to gold
With the slightest touch
Impregnating the Universe with Positive Action
There's nothing wrong with a little passion.
So while time is passing we are holding her close.
So close within her we are the host

The Whole Story

Other Cheudi Published Poetry

My Time to Speak
Clifford Leon Sheffield

God Is The Answer
Clifford Leon Sheffield

The Whole Story

The Whole Story

Since 2003
Cheudi Publishing,
Irving, Texas 75014